Tracing Through Theory

Volume One:
The Grand Staff

by Kimberly and Kurt Snow

Tracing Through Theory
Volume One: The Grand Staff

Eleven lessons to teach the beginner
music student the grand staff

Copyright 2019 Kurt and Kimberly Snow

www.TracingThroughTheory.com

ISBN 978-1493592128

Further works from Kurt & Kimberly Snow
Hymns for Kids: Learn How to Read and Enjoy Christian Hymns
Favorite Hymns for Kids
Just Hymns
www.PraiseNotes.com

Further works from Kurt Snow
Mr. Humdinger Goes Fishing (video for kids: www.MrHumdinger.com)
Patrick Biddle's Great Adventure (book for kids: www.PatrickBiddle.com)

Table of Contents

Forward

Many parents start their children in piano lessons around five to seven-years-old. With little or no musical training, the child's first lesson book should cover the basics, especially how to read music. But often that is not the case.

As a music teacher, I have found that the standard, popular beginner lesson books do not cover some key, basic concepts.

For example, it is much easier for a child to understand the grand staff if they first understand horizontal and vertical lines. And if you first teach a child about the spaces and lines of the grand staff, they can then more readily grasp where notes belong.

That is why I have written this workbook, which can be used as a supplement to any beginner lesson book.

Tracing Through Theory is the result of teaching many beginner students (some as young as five-years-old, but adults as well) how to play the piano, and implementing the concepts found in this book in my own piano studio.

The book begins with teaching about lines: horizontal lines, where space and line notes "live;" and vertical lines, which are used as bar lines and double bar lines. From there, it moves to the music staff, measures, braces, treble and bass clef, and more —all the elements to make the grand staff.

It is one thing to teach these concepts, it is, of course, another for the child to understand them. Teachers, no matter the subject, can attest to how often they teach a concept, and yet the student fails to grasp the lesson. Focus, repetition, and exercise are essential.

That is why this workbook is called *TRACING Through Theory*. In nearly every lesson, the child must trace the concept—trace the treble clef, bass clef, bar lines, whole notes, and more. At the concluding lesson, they make the connection between what they see on the grand staff to where they place their fingers on the keyboard. Students learn by doing.

I hope your students will move forward in their music studies as they "trace through theory."

Kimberly Snow

ELEMENTS OF THE GRAND STAFF

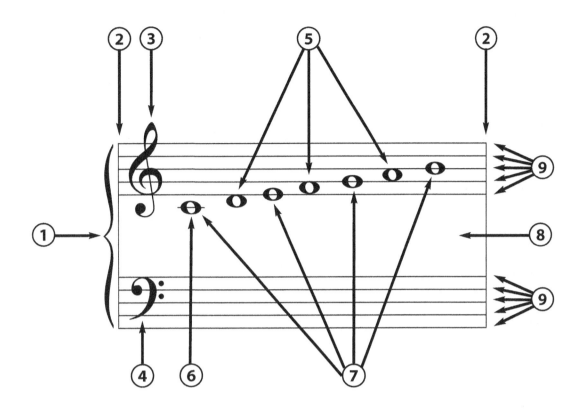

(1) Curly brace   (6) "Middle C" (ledger line)

(2) Single bar lines   (7) Line (whole) notes

(3) Treble clef   (8) Middle of staves

(4) Bass clef   (9) Staff lines

(5) Space (whole) notes

LESSON 1 — LINES AND THE MIDDLE

In This Lesson

- Horizontal Line
- Vertical Line
- The Middle

A horizontal line, like lying on your bed taking a snooze!

(**1**) A horizontal line is a parallel, straight line which moves from left to right across the page.

(**2**) A vertical line is a parallel, straight line which is placed in an up and down position.

(**3**) The middle is the center of something or the halfway point. In this example, the gray rectangle is in the middle and is between the top and bottom horizontal lines.

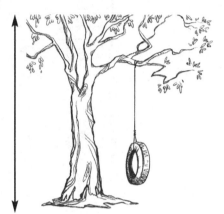

A vertical line, like a tree that grows straight up!

Horizontal lines move across the page

The gray rectangle is in the middle between the top and bottom horizontal lines.

Vertical lines move up and down

Complete the following exercises.

1 Circle the horizontal line.

Ⓐ 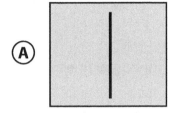   Ⓑ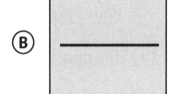

2 Circle the vertical line.

Ⓐ 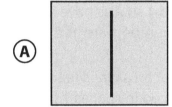   Ⓑ

3 Circle the line that is in the middle of the square shape.

Ⓐ    Ⓑ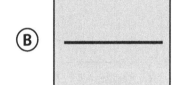

4 Circle the 5 horizontal lines.

Ⓐ    Ⓑ

5 Circle the 2 shapes below which have vertical lines.

Ⓐ   Ⓑ   Ⓒ   Ⓓ

      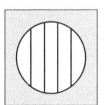   

LESSON 2 — THE MUSIC STAFF

In This Lesson

- The Music Staff
- 5 Horizontal Lines
- 4 Spaces Between the 5 Lines
- Whole Notes

What does a whole note look like?
Answer: Drawn on the music staff it looks like a chicken egg with a black outline.

(1) The music staff has 5 horizontal lines.

(2) There are 4 spaces between the 5 horizontal lines.

(3) Each of the 5 lines and 4 spaces have a number. The lowest number (1) is at the bottom, the highest numbers are at the top.

(4) Notes are symbols that musicians read on the music staff. The example below shows four whole notes[1] placed in spaces 1 through 4.

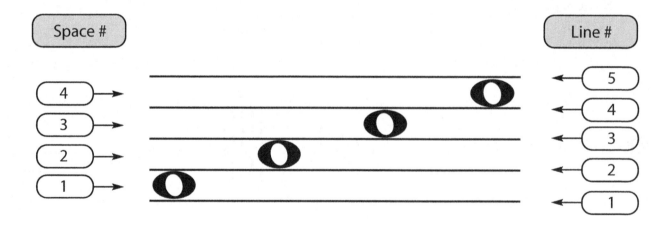

[1] Note values are addressed in Tracing Through Theory: Volume 2

WORKSHEET 2

Complete the following exercises.

1 Number each of the 5 horizontal lines beginning with line 1.

2 Number each of the 4 spaces between the 5 horizontal lines beginning with line 1.

3 Trace over the 5 dashed horizontal lines using 5 different colored markers beginning with line 1.

4 What do the four whole notes found in the spaces look like? Circle the correct answer.

    A. White notes with a black outline, or a chicken egg with a black outline

    B. Black notes with a white outline

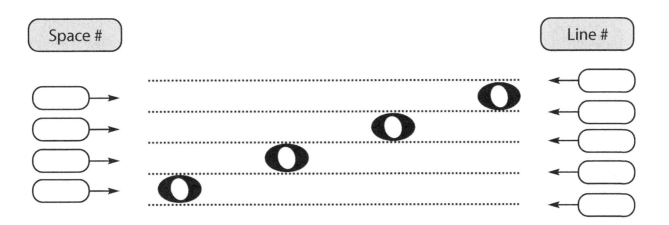

LESSON 3 — MUSIC STAVES

This is not a music staff in my hand!

In This Lesson
- Music Staves
- Space Notes
- Line Notes

(1) When there is more than one music staff, it is called staves.

(2) Music notes can be placed on any horizontal line or any space on the music staff.

(3) Space notes touch a line either on top or below the note, or it can touch both lines. In the staff group 1 example, whole notes are in spaces 1 through 4. Space notes do not have a line through their middle.

(4) Lines notes have a line through the middle of the note. Staff group 2 is an example of line notes. There are whole notes on each of the 5 lines of the music staff.

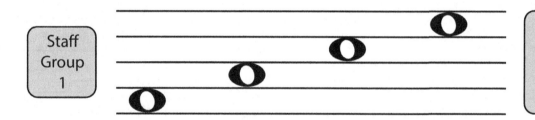

Staff Group 1

Space notes touch a line above or below the note

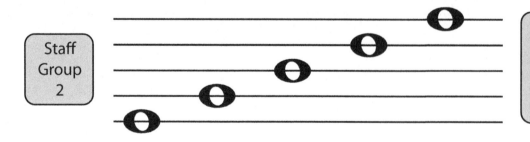

Staff Group 2

Line notes have lines through the middle of the note

Complete the following exercises.

1 Circle the space note on the 4th space in staff group 1.

2 Circle the line note on the 1st line in staff group 2.

Circle the correct answers.

3 When there is more than one music staff they are called:

      A. Staff lines   B. Staves

4 Staff Group 1 contains what kind of whole notes?

      A. Line notes   B. Space notes

5 A line note has a line through the middle of the note.

      A. True   B. False

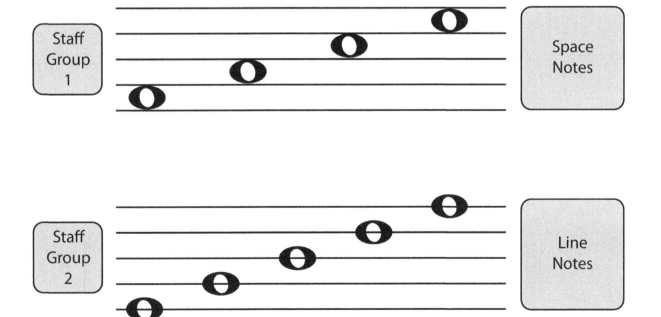

LESSON 4 — BAR LINES AND MEASURES

In This Lesson

- Bar Lines
- Measures

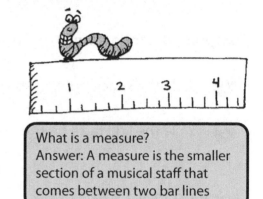

(1) A single staff or a group of staves can be divided into sections by using vertical lines called bar lines. Bar lines are vertical lines that connect line 1 to line 5 in a single staff, or they connect staves together.

> What is a measure?
> Answer: A measure is the smaller section of a musical staff that comes between two bar lines

(2) Example A shows two types of bar lines. A single, thin bar line breaks up the music into smaller groups called measures. The bar line at the end of the song is a double bar line. It has two bar lines. The first is thin, the second is thick.

(A) A single, thin bar line marks the start of a measure

A double bar line (the first thin, the last thick) marks the end of the song

(3) Bar lines are used to separate the music into measures. In example B, the single barlines have divided the music into 3 measures. The final measure (measure 3) has a double bar line at the end.

(B) | Measure 1 | Measure 2 | Measure 3 |

WORKSHEET 4

Complete the following exercises.

1 Trace over the single and double bar lines with color 1.

2 Trace over the 10 horizontal staff lines with color 2.

3 Write the line numbers 1, 2, 3, 4 and 5 in staff group 1 and staff group 2.

4 Trace over the 10 whole notes on each of the lines with color 3.

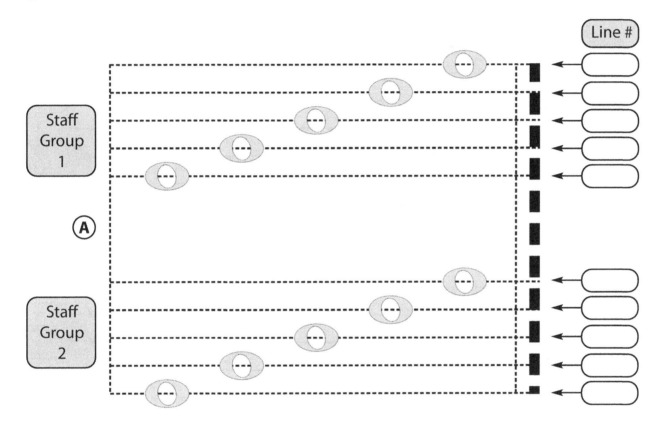

5 Circle the measure that has the final double bar line.

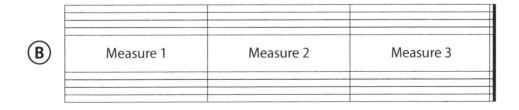

LESSON 5 — CURLY BRACE

In This Lesson

- Brace

(1) A curly brace joins or connects two or more music staffs.

(2) A curly brace is placed in front of the first bar line.

(3) When 2 staffs are used together they are called the Grand Staff.

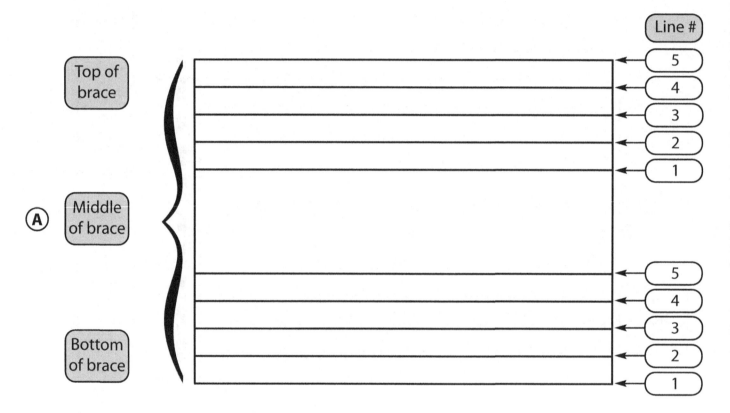

(4) A curly brace may stretch up or down to allow the middle section (gray) to become smaller or larger as seen in examples B, C and D.

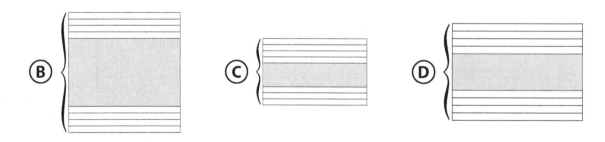

Complete the following exercises.

1 Circle the picture with the longest curly brace.

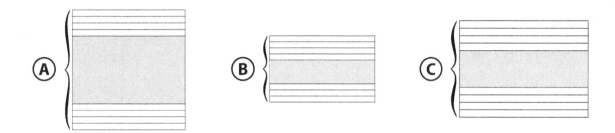

2 Beginning at the top of the curly brace, trace down to the bottom with color 1.

3 Trace over the two bar lines with color 2.

4 Write the correct numbers, 1 or 2, in the correct staff group circles.

5 Write the correct numbers in the spaces provided for the line numbers.

LESSON 6 — TREBLE CLEF

In This Lesson

- Treble Clef Sign
- Line 2

(1) The treble clef is a sign drawn on the top 5 staff lines (see staff group 1 below). To remember where the treble clef belongs, think of "**T**" as in **T**reble for **T**op staff lines.

(2) The treble clef sign ends by wrapping around line 2.

"T' for Top ... like a top hat!

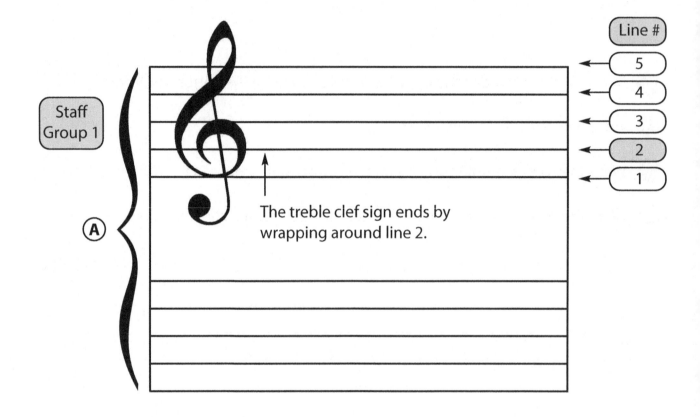

Staff Group 1

A

The treble clef sign ends by wrapping around line 2.

Line #
5
4
3
2
1

(3) Treble clef signs are placed at the left-hand side of the first measure as shown in example B.

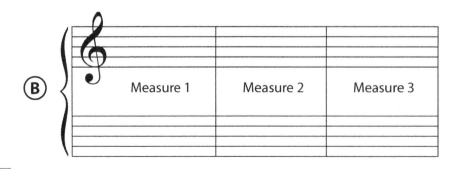

B | Measure 1 | Measure 2 | Measure 3

Trace the treble clef in staff group 1 in example A below by following these 3 steps.

For more treble clefs to trace, see page 27.

1

Start at the top of the treble clef and trace down the center line that looks like an umbrella handle.

2

Starting back at the top of the treble clef, trace the curve to the right of the center line and cross over the center line.

3

Continue tracing to the left of the center line and continuing around the curve to the end.

Staff Group 1

Line #

5
4
3
2
1

A

LESSON 7 — BASS CLEF

In This Lesson

- Bass Clef Sign
- Line 4

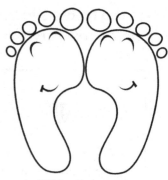

(1) The bass clef sign is on the bottom 5 staff lines (see staff group 2 in example A). To remember where the bass clef belongs, think "**B**" as in **B**ass for **B**ottom staff lines.

(2) The bass clef sign starts on line 4. The last two dots are put above and below line 4.

"B" for Bottom ...
like the bottom of your feet!

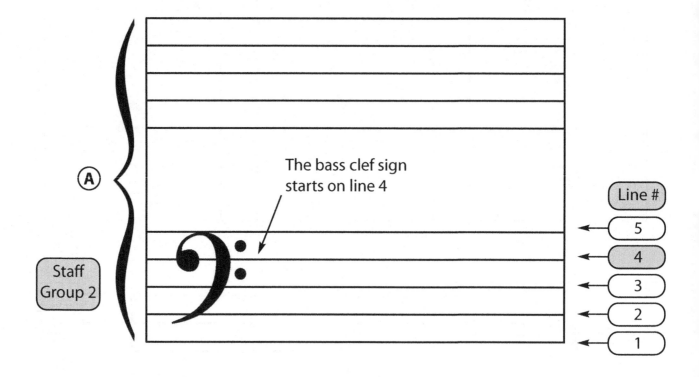

The bass clef sign starts on line 4

(A)

Staff Group 2

Line #
5
4
3
2
1

(3) Bass clef signs are placed at the left-hand side of the first measure, as shown in Example B.

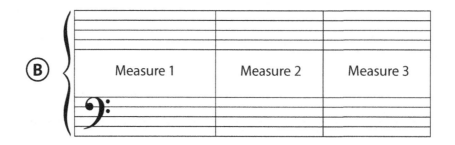

(B)

Measure 1   Measure 2   Measure 3

WORKSHEET 7

Trace the bass clef in staff group 2 in example A below by following these 3 steps.

For more treble clefs to trace, see page 28.

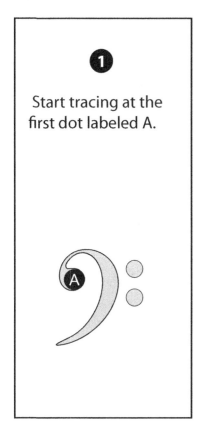

1 Start tracing at the first dot labeled A.

2 Continue tracing up and around the curve to the end of the sign.

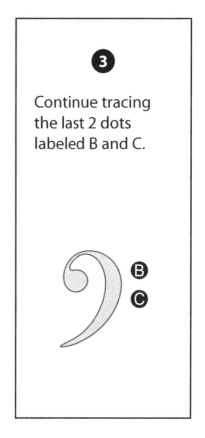

3 Continue tracing the last 2 dots labeled B and C.

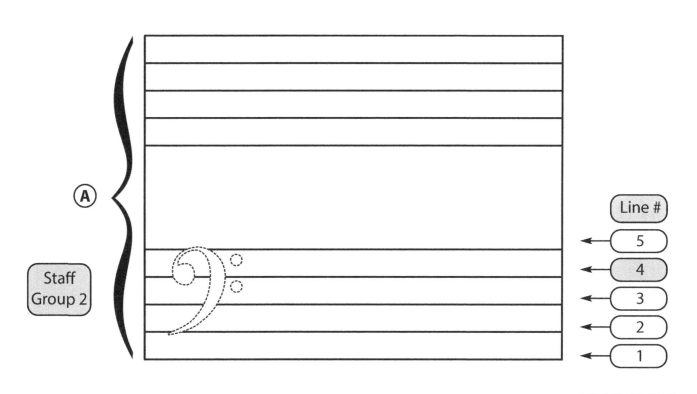

Page 16

LESSON 8 — THE MIDDLE

In This Lesson

- The Middle of the Grand Staff
- 2 Middle Space Notes and 1 Middle Line Note
- Ledger Lines

The middle, like your nose in the middle of your face

(1) The grand staff has 3 sections: 1) staff group 1, the treble clef; 2) staff group 2, the bass clef; and, 3) The middle. (Example A)

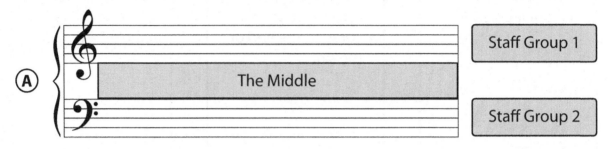

(A) The Middle

Staff Group 1

Staff Group 2

(2) The middle looks empty, but it is not! There is an "invisible" line that runs through the middle of the middle, below the treble clef, and above the bass clef. (Example B)

(3) The middle section, just like staff groups 1 and 2, has both space notes and line notes. There are two space notes—one above and one below the invisible line—and one line note. (Example B)

(4) If there are no notes in the middle, the line remains hidden. If there are notes, then the line appears. But the invisible line only shows through the line note called "Middle C," which we will learn about in lesson 10. (Example C)

(5) If there are notes in the middle section, then the lines that are now visible are called ledger lines. (Example C)

The "invisible" line

Ledger line

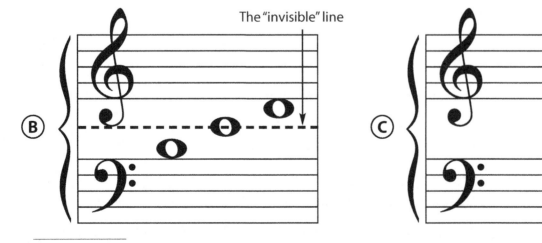

(B)

(C)

WORKSHEET 8

Complete the following exercises.

1 Label the 3 sections of the grand staff below (refer to example A on page 18).

a. Staff group 1, the _____ clef

b. The _____ of the grand staff

c. Staff group 2, the _____ clef

2 The middle section in example A below has ... (circle the correct answer)

a. 2 space notes and 1 line note   b. 2 line notes and 1 space note

3 The notes in the grand staff below (example A) are found in which section? (circle the correct answer).

a. Staff group 1   b. Staff group 2   c. The middle

4 In example A below, circle the note with the ledger line ("Middle C").

5 Trace over the note and ledger line in example B below.

LESSON 9 — KEYS AND THE KEYBOARD

In This Lesson

- Keys
- Keyboard

(1) The piano has keys. When you press a key, it makes a sound called a tone. The keys have two colors: white and black.

(2) Each white key has a name. The names are letters. There are only 7 names and they are the first 7 letters of the alphabet: A, B, C, D, E, F and G. (See example A)

(A)

(3) Each group of 5 black keys are divided into two groups. The first group has 2 black keys; the second group has 3 black keys. This pattern repeats across the keyboard. (See example B)

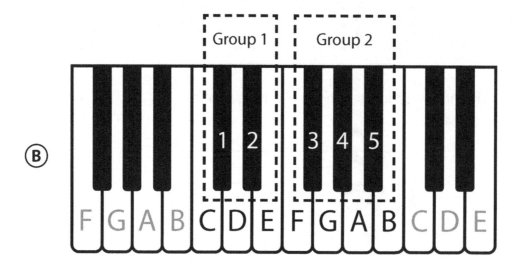

(B)

Complete the following exercises.

Circle the correct answers.

1 What are the two colors of piano keys?

1. Blue   2. White   3. Black   4. Green

2 What are the 7 letter names found on the keyboard?

1. H, I, J, K, L, M, N   2. A, B, C, D, E, F, G   3. T, U V, W, X, Y, Z

3 How many black keys are found between "C" and "B"?

1. Six   2. Four   3. Five

4 Circle all the groups of 2 black keys in one color. Using a different color, circle all the groups of the 3 black keys. For more practice, see page 29.

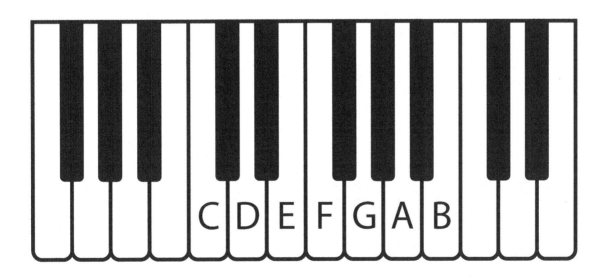

LESSON 10 — MIDDLE C

In This Lesson

- Middle C

Do you see "C"?

(1) There are more than one "C" key on the keyboard. How do you find the "C"s? They are always the white key next to the two black keys, on the left-hand side.

(2) As we learned in Lesson 8, an invisible line runs through the middle section of the grand staff. If there is a note in the middle, then the invisible line appears as a ledger line and runs through the middle of the note. This note is Middle "C" (example A).

(3) Middle "C" is in the middle of the keyboard (example B).

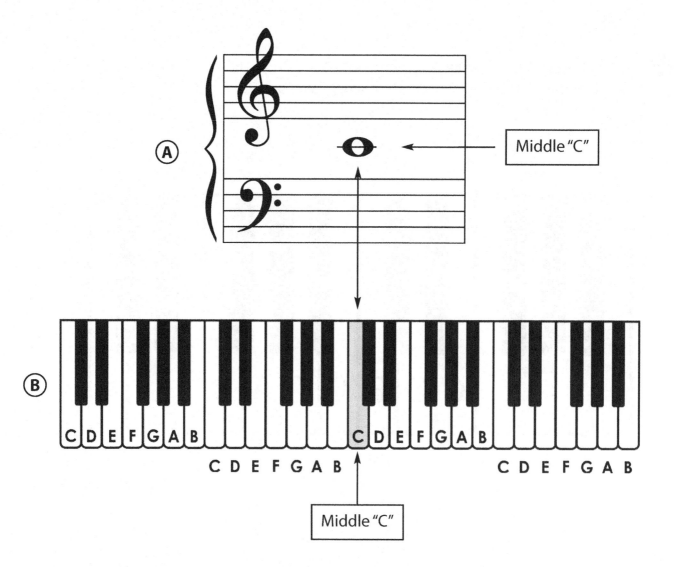

Complete the following exercises.

1 Write all the "C"s on the keyboard, then color the "Middle C" key with color 1. Color all the other "C"s with color 2.

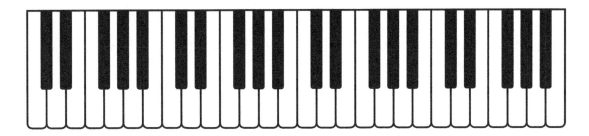

Circle the correct answer.

2 Middle C is found where on the grand staff?

1. Treble clef staff lines   2. Bass clef staff lines   3. In the middle of the grand staff

3 Does "Middle C" have a line that runs through it?

1. Yes   2. No

4 What is that line called?

1. Staff line   2. Ledger line   3. Bar line

5 Draw a "Middle C" note on the ledger line below

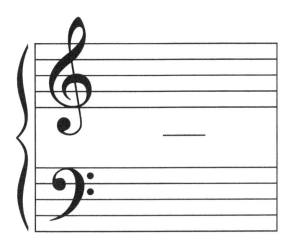

LESSON 11 — NOTES AND KEYS

In This Lesson

- Connecting Notes to Keys

(1) Each line note or space note on the staff lines tells the musician which key to press on the keyboard.

(2) The names of the notes on the staff lines have the same names of the key you press on the keyboard.

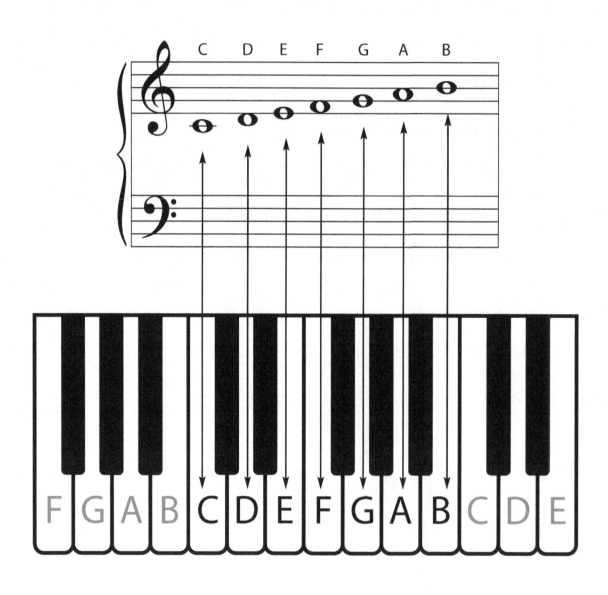

WORKSHEET 11

Complete the following exercises.

1 Write the letter names of the notes in the correct box above the treble clef.

2 Write the letter names on the keyboard in example B below.

3 Trace along the dotted line from the note on the treble clef staff lines to the matching key on the keyboard.

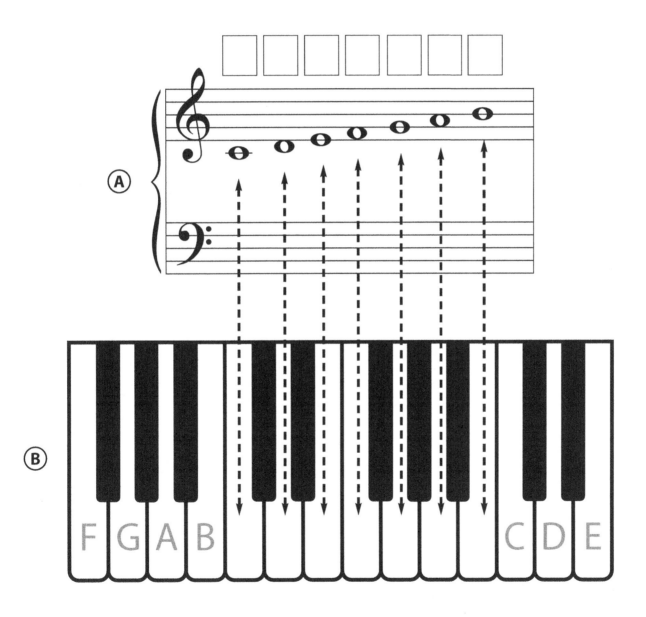

EXTRA WORKSHEET #1 — MUSIC TERMS

Draw a line from the music term on the left to the matching graphic on the right.

(1) Treble Clef

(2) Staves

(3) Bar lines

(4) Staff

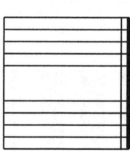

(5) Brace

(6) Bass Clef

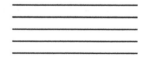

EXTRA WORKSHEET #2 — TREBLE CLEF

Trace over each treble clef, following the instructions on page 15.

EXTRA WORKSHEET #3 — BASS CLEF

Trace over each bass clef, following the instructions on page 17.

EXTRA WORKSHEET #4 — THE KEYBOARD

1 Write the 7 letters of the musical names C, D, E, F, G, A and B on the white keys.

2 Highlight each white key with a different color. Each keyboard should have 7 different colors when you are finished.

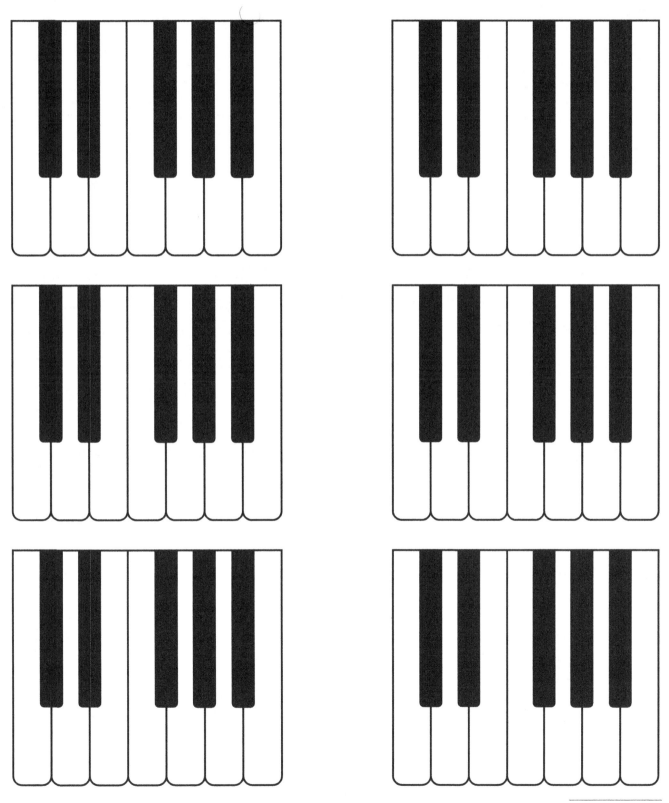

ANSWER KEY — WORKSHEET 1

Complete the following exercises.

1 Circle the horizontal line.

(A) 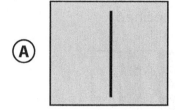   (B)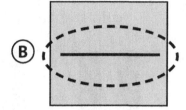

2 Circle the vertical line.

(A) 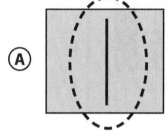   (B)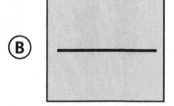

3 Circle the line that is in the middle of the square shape.

(A) 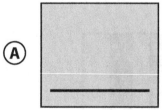   (B)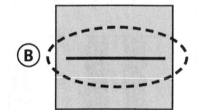

4 Circle the 5 horizontal lines.

(A)    (B)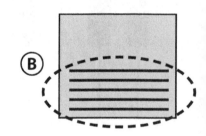

5 Circle the 2 shapes below which have vertical lines.

(A)    (B)    (C) 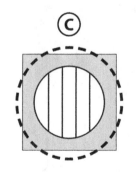   (D)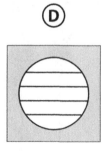

Complete the following exercises.

1 Number each of the 5 lines beginning with line 1.

2 Number each of the 4 spaces beginning with line 1.

3 Trace over the 5 dashed lines using 5 different colored markers beginning with line 1.

4 What do the whole notes found in the spaces look like? Circle the correct answer.

A. White notes with a black outline, or a chicken egg with a black outline

B. Black notes with a white outline

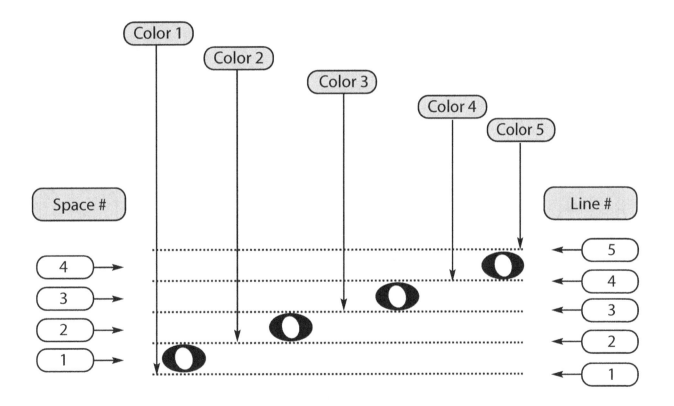

ANSWER KEY — WORKSHEET 3

Complete the following exercises.

1 Circle the space note on the 4th space in staff group 1.

2 Circle the line note on the 1st line in staff group 2.

Circle the correct answers.

3 When there is more than one music staff they are called:

      A. Staff lines   (B. Staves)

4 Staff Group 1 contains what kind of whole notes?

      A. Line notes   (B. Space notes)

5 A line note has a line through the middle of the note.

      (A. True)   B. False

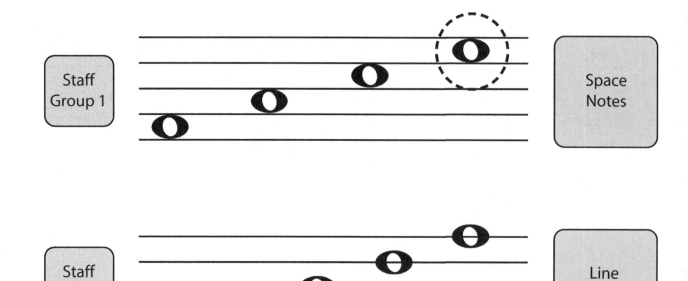

ANSWER KEY — WORKSHEET 4

Complete the following exercises.

1 Trace over the single and double bar lines with color 1.

2 Trace over the 10 horizontal staff lines with color 2.

3 Write the line numbers 1, 2, 3, 4 and 5 in staff group 1 and staff group 2.

4 Trace over the 10 whole notes on each of the lines.

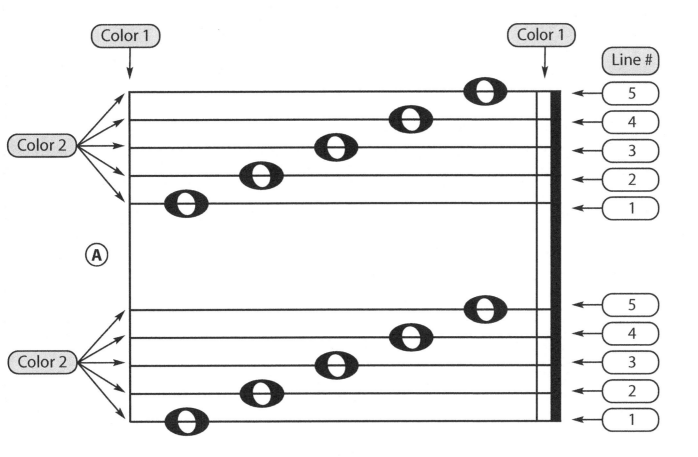

5 Circle the measure that has the final double bar line.

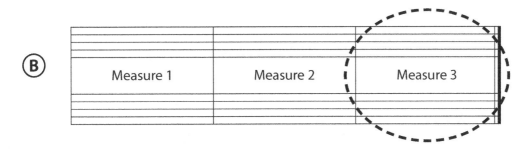

ANSWER KEY — WORKSHEET 5

Complete the following exercises.

1 Circle the picture with the longest curly brace.

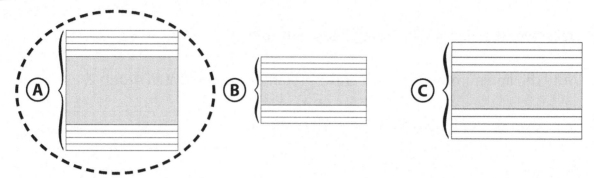

2 Beginning at the top of the curly brace, trace down to the bottom with color 1.

3 Trace over the two bar lines with color 2.

4 Write the correct number, 1 or 2, in the correct staff group circles.

5 Write the correct numbers in the spaces provided for the line numbers.

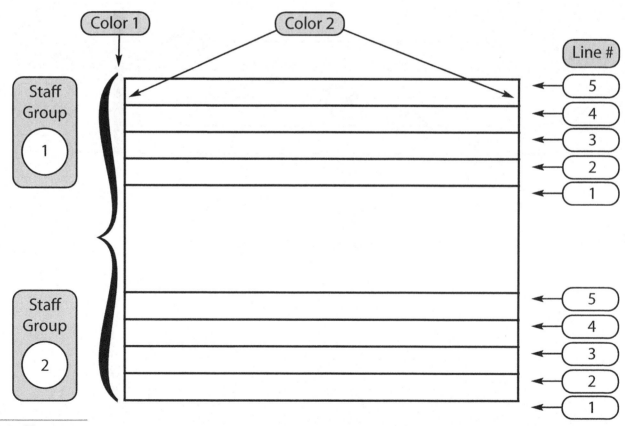

ANSWER KEY — WORKSHEET 6

Trace the treble clef in staff group 1 in example A below by following these 3 steps.

Start at the top of the treble clef and trace down the center line that looks like an umbrella handle.

Starting back at the top of the treble clef, trace the curve to the right of the center line and cross over the center line.

Continue tracing to the left of the center line and continuing around the curve to the end.

Line #

Staff Group 1

5
4
3
2
1

A

ANSWER KEY — WORKSHEET 7

Trace the bass clef in staff group 2 in example A below by following these 3 steps.

1

Start tracing at the first circle labeled A.

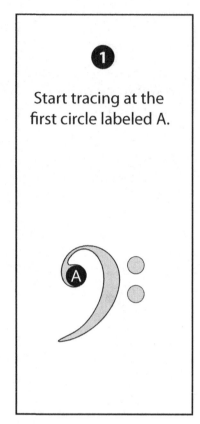

2

Continue tracing up and around the curve to the end of the sign.

3

Continue tracing the last 2 dots labeled B and C.

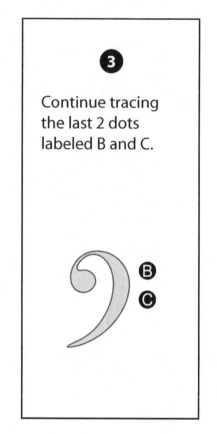

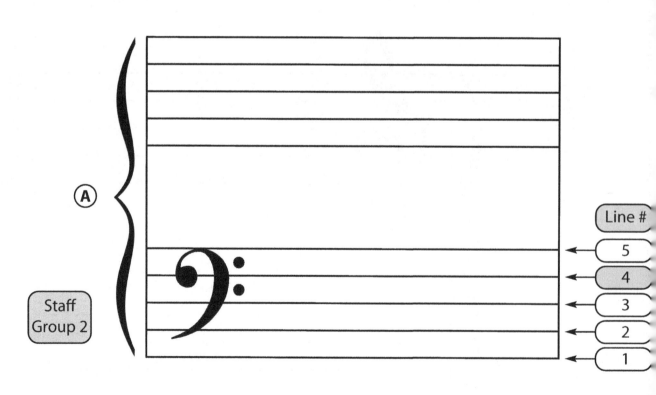

Ⓐ

Staff Group 2

Line #

5
4
3
2
1

Complete the following exercises.

1 Label the 3 sections of the grand staff below (use example A on page 18).

   a. Staff Group 1, the <u>treble</u> clef

   b. The <u>middle</u> of the grand staff

   c. Staff Group 2, the <u>bass</u> clef

2 The middle section in example A below has ... (Circle the correct answer)

   (a. 2 space notes and 1 line note)   b. 2 line notes and 1 space note

3 The notes in the grand staff below (example A) are found in which section? (circle the correct answer).

   a. Staff group 1   b. Staff group 2   (c. The middle)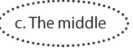

4 In example A below, circle the note with the ledger line ("Middle C").

5 Trace over the note and ledger line in example B below.

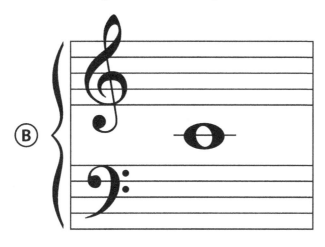

ANSWER KEY — WORKSHEET 9

Complete the following exercises.

Circle the correct answers.

1 What are the two colors of piano keys?

1. Blue   (2. White)   (3. Black)   4. Green

2 What are the 7 letter names found on the keyboard?

1. H, I, J, K, L, M, N   (2. A, B, C, D, E, F, G)   3. T, U V, W, X, Y, Z

3 How many black keys are found within one group?

1. Six   2. Four   (3. Five)

4 Circle all the groups of 2 black keys in one color. Using a different color, circle all the groups of the 3 black keys. For more practice, see page 29.

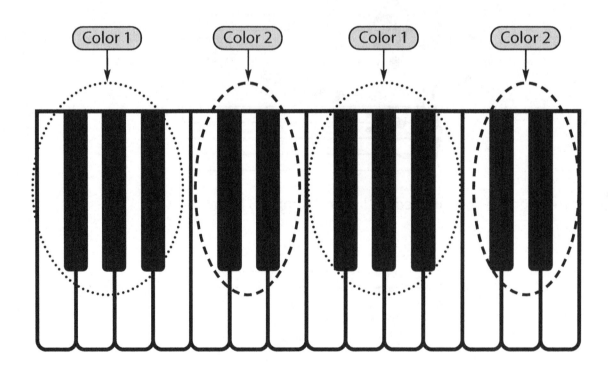

ANSWER KEY — WORKSHEET 10

Complete the following exercises.

1 Write all the "C"s on the keyboard, then color the "Middle C" key with color 1. Color all the other "C"s with color 2.

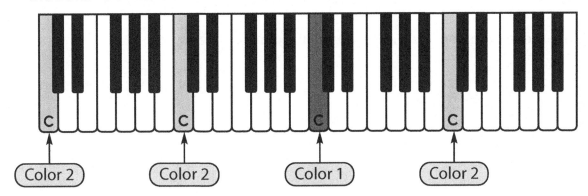

Color 2   Color 2   Color 1   Color 2

Circle the correct answer.

2 Middle C is found where on the grand staff?

1. On the treble clef   2. On the bass clef   *3. In the middle of the grand staff*

3 Does "Middle C" have a line that runs through it?

1. Yes   2. No

4 What is that line called?

1. Staff line   *2. Ledger line*   3. Bar line

5 Draw a "Middle C" note on the ledger line below

ANSWER KEY — WORKSHEET 11

Complete the following exercises.

1 Write the names of the notes on the grand staff in the correct box above the treble clef.

2 Write the letter names on the keyboard in example B below.

3 Trace along the dotted line from the note on the treble clef to the matching note on the keyboard.

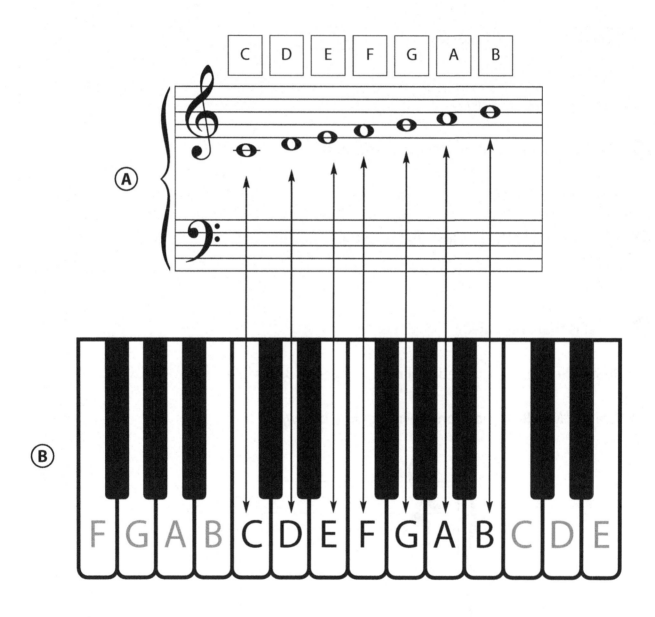

ANSWER KEY — EXTRA WORKSHEET #1

Draw a line from the music term to the matching graphic.

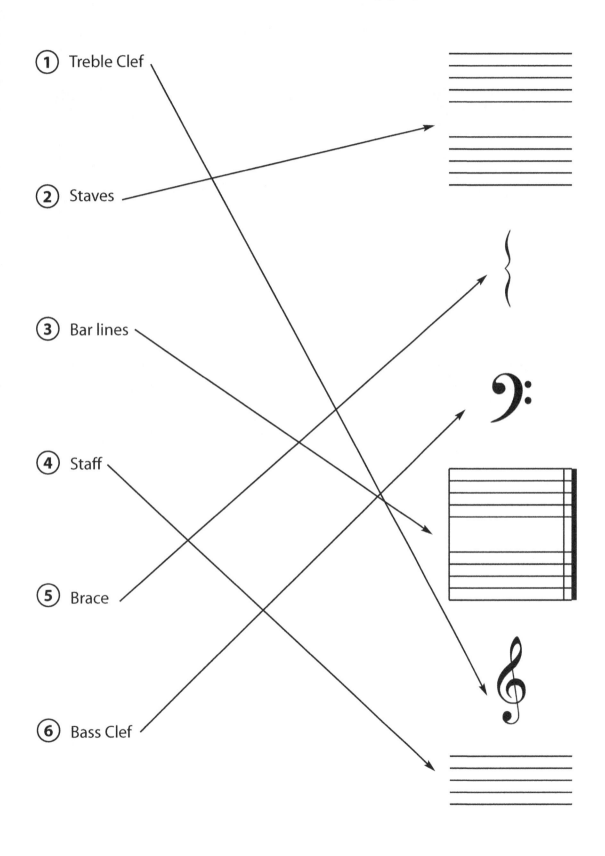

ANSWER KEY — EXTRA WORKSHEET #4

1 Write the 7 letters of the musical names A, B, C, D, E, F, and G on the white keys.

2 Highlight each white key with a different color. Each keyboard should have 7 different colors when you are finished.

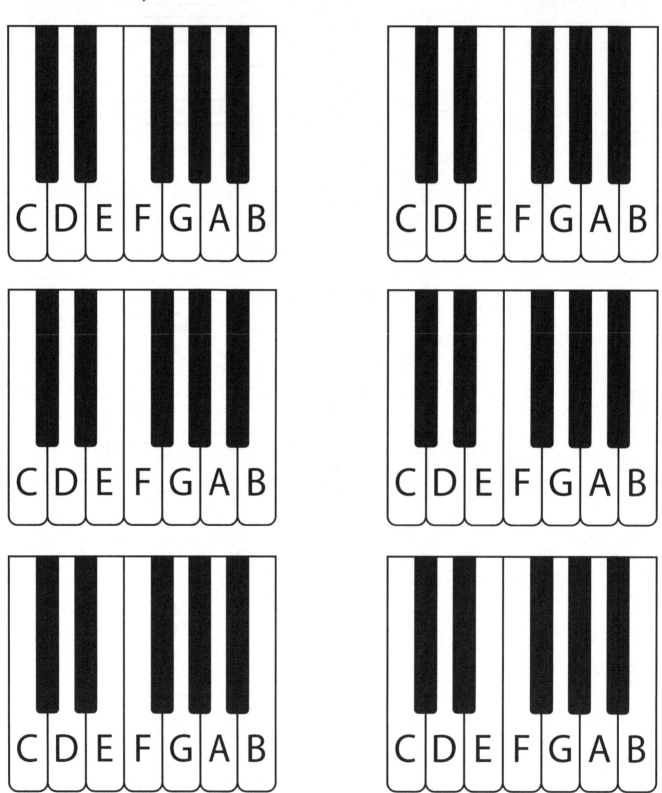

GLOSSARY

Horizontal Line	A parallel, straight line which moves from left to right across the page.
Vertical Line	A parallel, straight line which is placed in an up and down position.
Bass Clef	A sign used inside the grand staff. It represents notes on the grand staff and keys on the piano below Middle C.
Curly Brace	A curly brace is used to connect two or more staffs together. It is placed in front of the first bar line.
Grand Staff	The total of 11 horizontal lines, brace, treble and bass clefs, and bar lines that musicians use to read music.
Keyboard	A set of keys on a piano or similar musical instrument.
Keyboard Names	There are seven names which are repeated across the keyboard. The names are the first seven letters of the alphabet A, B, C, D, E, F, and G.
Ledger Line	A short horizontal line added for notes above or below the range of a staff.
Line Notes	Notes that have a line going through the middle section of the note.
Measure	The smaller section of a musical staff that comes between two bar lines.
Middle C	A note found in the middle of the grand staff when reading music. Middle C has a ledger line running through the middle of the note.
Space Notes	Notes that do not have a line going through the middle section of the note.
Staff	The music staff has 5 horizontal lines. There are 4 spaces between the 5 horizontal lines. Each of the 5 lines and 4 spaces have a number. The lowest number (1) is at the bottom, the highest numbers are at the top.
Staves	When there is more than one music staff it is called staves.
Treble Clef	A sign used in the grand staff. It represents notes on the grand staff and keys on the piano above Middle C.

Certificate
of Completion

This Certificate of Completing
Tracing Through Theory:
The Grand Staff

is presented to

_____

NAME

_____

DATE

ABOUT THE AUTHORS

Kimberly Snow has been teaching piano students for over 20 years. As a piano teacher, she discovered that the music curriculum using hymns was limited and difficult for beginner music students to play. To address this need, Kimberly began studying hymnology, music theory, and composition. Soon, she started writing arrangements of hundreds of the most popular hymns of the Christian faith. She integrates many concepts—including the Circle of Fifths, improvisation, and chord stylization—to help the student understand music and how to play the hymns. Her arrangements and other products are available on her website at PraiseNotes.com.

Kimberly has also been a church musician for over 25 years. She loves teaching online piano lessons across the country via Zoom. The national publications, "The Church Pianist" and Lorenz's piano solos for Holy Week, "With Jesus Through the Shadows," have published her advanced hymn arrangements.

Kurt Snow, along with his wife, Kimberly, compose hymns, praise worship music, and songs for children's choirs. Together, they have written the books *Hymns for Kids*, *Tracing Through Theory*, and *Lickety-Split Music Drills*. He produced the educational, comedy video for 3-7 year-old children, *Mr. Humdinger Goes Fishing*, which aired on PBS, and wrote *Patrick Biddle's Great Adventure*, a novel for 8-12 year-olds. He is the webmaster for the couple's websites and a graphic layout artist, working in the advertising industry.

A personal note from Kimberly

Like so many other children, I begged my parents to let me quit piano lessons. After I complained enough, they finally gave in. I eventually returned to piano lessons as a young adult. Not long after taking lessons, our church pianist moved away, and there was no one to take her place...except me. Thus, I began the journey that has led to my work on music theory.

Playing for the church motivated me to practice and practice, then practice some more. It also drove me to the studios of several dedicated, professional pianists. All of them taught me something new, something valuable. In addition to piano performance, I continued to study theory and became interested in music composition.

I first taught my own children how to play the piano, and soon other parents asked me to teach their children. As I began this journey, I discovered that students often do not understand the most basic music concepts, like staff lines (which make up both horizontal and vertical lines—something a young child usually does not grasp), space notes, line notes, and so on. I tried many different standard, popular beginner music workbooks. Still, too often, they skipped vital concepts, and my students were not progressing. As I began studying music theory, I was also writing original compositions and arranging dozens of songs for my students. The exercise of putting my music theory training to practical use helped me to understand and master many concepts. It helped me to integrate what I had learned of music theory, especially the principles of the Circle of Fifths, into my piano studio. These principles helped my students to not only better play their assigned pieces but also gave them the foundation to begin composing their own songs and playing their own arrangements. I have found that students enjoy the piano so much more when they understand the principles undergirding what they are practicing and can apply those principles to their own creative work. I have learned something wonderful: students at all levels can create their own arrangements and compose their own songs once they grasp and apply music theory.

Tracing Through Theory's
Lickety-Split Music Drills

Kids like to go fast. They like to run as fast they can; they like to ride roller coasters; they like to play fast games—and they like music speed drills. *Tracing Through Theory's Lickety-Split Music Drills* will help the beginner music student more quickly identify note names and accurately play notes in the treble and bass clefs. Tracing Through Theory's Lickety-Split Music Drills includes:

- 72-speed drills—36 in the treble clef; 36 in the bass clef.

- Written and played speed drills. In the written portion of the speed drill, the student identifies and fills in the name of the note. The played speed drill tests how quickly the student can play the notes.

- Word game worksheets. The student fills in the letter name of the note in the blank line. The notes in each measure spell out a word, like "egg," "face," "add," and so forth. The student will enjoy figuring out what word is "hidden" in each measure as they practice identifying each note's name.

- Answer keys

Students love these drills and progress more quickly in their recognition of notes, as well as in playing their assigned piano pieces when speed drills are a routine part of their lessons and practice.

For more information, and to review sample pages and drills, please visit our website: www.TracingThroughTheory.com.

Hymns for Kids

Learn How to Read and Enjoy Christian Hymns
(Psalms and Praise Choruses, Too!)

Hymns for Kids teaches children about worship music, concentrating on hymns. Along the way, they learn many key musical concepts as they learn how to "read" a hymn. It is designed to be used with our *Favorite Hymns for Kids* series.

Although this book was written for children, it is helpful for any person (especially teachers) who are interested in learning about and teaching Christian hymns. The book is divided into four parts: an overview of hymns; the "technical stuff"; *Hymns for Kids* hymnal; and, worksheets, puzzles and answer keys.

Overview
- The reason why we sing and what the Bible has to say about singing
- The history and purpose of hymns
- Types of worship songs: psalms, hymns and modern praise songs
- A review of famous hymns and hymnbooks
- A review of some famous hymn writers like Isaac Watts and Fanny Crosby

The "Technical Stuff"
- How many people does it take to write a hymn?
- Voices; four part harmonies
- Lyrics and refrains
- Tune names
- Meters: common, long, short, etc.
- How to use a hymnbook

The Second Edition includes:
- Over 50 "Quick Review" questions
- New section on the Psalms
- Special words found in hymns: Amen and Alleluia
- Special types of hymns: Benedictions, Doxologies, Musical Responses (*Amen, Gloria Patri*, and more)
- Hymns for Kids Hymnal: representation of what a hymnal looks like; indexes
- Worksheets, puzzles and answer keys

For more information, or to order, visit www.PraiseNotes.com

Just Hymns

Just Hymns is a series of Kim Snow's simple, easy hymn arrangements for piano students. The arrangements are appropriate for any beginner, regardless of age. *Just Hymns* includes easy piano arrangements, and piano arrangement marks reference sheet, and glossary. *Just Hymns* does not include hymn worksheets, rhythm worksheets, and hymn and rhythm worksheet answer keys. Each *Just Hymns* book include:

Piano Arrangements
- Enlarged music score—two pages per hymn
- Verse one of the hymn, additional marks including introduction, refrain, playing both hands up one octave and final "Amen" ending
- Measure numbers (circled) at the beginning of each music scoreline
- Arrows for re-positioning fingers

Other Features
- Piano arrangement marks reference sheet
- Rhythm worksheet reference sheet
- Glossary

Favorite Hymns for Kids

"Favorite Hymns for Kids" is a series of Kim Snow's piano hymn arrangements for piano students. Combining easy arrangements, instructions on how to "read" a hymn and music theory, "Favorite Hymns" is a proven method to train beginner students not only how to play the hymns on the piano, but also to develop a love for hymns and learn the great truths of the Christian faith. "Favorite Hymns" is available in four series: popular hymns, Christmas, Easter, and Thanksgiving. Each book includes:

Arrangement
- Enlarged music score—two pages per hymn
- Lyrics for verse one
- Key signature/scale
- Measure numbers
- Finger numbers for both hands
- Arrows for re-positioning fingers

Student Hymn Worksheets
- Hymn name and Tune name
- Hymn meter
- Key signature
- Time signature
- Music practice check-off list
- Additional hymn verses

For more information, and to review sample pages, please visit our website:

PraiseNotes.com

Mr. Humdinger Goes Fishing

As seen on PBS, Mr. Humdinger Goes Fishing is a live-action video that shows kids what it is like to be a commercial fisherman for a day.

Mr. Humdinger and his puppet sidekick, Mr. Fin, learn about the fishing industry from Captain Emery, skipper of a 90-foot fishing boat. Together, they learn about boats and safety equipment, visit the ice house and dry dock, and take the fishing vessel out to sea to catch some fish. Upon their return, they deliver their catch to the processing plant where it is prepared for the grocery store. While on the "job" Mr. Humdinger and Mr. Fin have all sorts of comical misadventures: Mr. Humdinger learns what it is like to eat on the ocean while making banana soup; Mr. Fin hijacks a fishing boat to search for the perfect fishburger; Mr. Humdinger discovers fishing is very hard work while scrubbing the deck with a toothbrush; Mr. Fin is accidentally sucked up the processing plant's hose; and on and on!

The National Parenting Center wrote: "If your child loves boats, the sea going, fishing kind, then they will enjoy learning more about how these boats take to the seas. In this video, which talks exclusively to the very youngest viewers, Mr. Humdinger bounces around the ship playing parts that are equally goofy and informative. This was the right mix for our young testers who were laughing and learning and gave the video … a thumbs up review."

For children 2-7 years old. For more information, or to order, visit www.MrHumdinger.com.

Patrick Biddle's Great Adventure

When Aunt Liddle visits ten-year-old Patrick Biddle, she unknowingly brings along a hitchhiking ant from Scotland … ornery, overly-dramatic, yet kind-hearted, Lutz McCoon. Before Lutz continues on to visit his relations at the ant colony in the Biddle's backyard, he and Patrick become friends. When Lutz McCoon discovers that all is not right in the colony, he remembers his friend and returns to seek his help. Patrick is magically shrunk, and enters an amazing underground world—a place filled with thousands of ants zigzagging on scooters, bicycles, cars, and trucks across thirty lanes of the Queen's Highway; where Mr. Garble's Grocery Store is stocked with fly guts; where the Garbage Police keeps everything spotless. After settling in, Patrick is assigned as a scout to help defend the colony. Despite his anxieties, he slowly gains confidence as he passes each challenge, including outwitting Smilk, a spider intent on eating Patrick.

His newfound skills, and the lessons he has learned, are put to a final severe test when he finally meets the colony's archenemy: Sotrick. Little does Patrick know that Sotrick is not only menacing, devious and smart, but he is also leading a secret army intent upon conquering the colony. Will Patrick pass the ultimate test?

Kids report that they love Patrick Biddle: "Patrick Biddle's Great Adventure is one of the funniest books I have ever read. There wasn't a chapter that I read that I didn't laugh at."

For children 8-12 years old. For more information or to order, visit www.PatrickBiddle.com.

Made in the USA
Monee, IL
08 February 2021